Critical Skills Needed to Be a Strategic Thinker

Title Page

Strategic Thinking
Mapping Out The Route To Success

Brice Alvord

Limits of Liability Disclaimer of Warranty

The author and publisher of this book and the accompanying materials have used their best efforts in preparing this program. The authors and publisher make no representation or warranties with respect to (the accuracy, applicability. fitness, or completeness of the contents of this program. They disclaim any warranties expressed or implied), merchantability, or fitness for any particular purpose. The authors and publisher shall in no event beheld liable for any loss or other damages, including but not limited to special, incidental, consequential, or other damages. As always, the advice of a competent legal, tax, accounting or other professional should be sought. The author and publisher do not warrant the performance, effectiveness, or applicability of any sites listed in this book. All links are for information purposes only and are not warranted for content, accuracy or any other implied or explicit purpose.

This book contains material protected under International and Federal Copyright Laws and Treaties. Any unauthorized reprint or use of this material is prohibited.

ALERA Publishing Group
PO Box 6111
Wyomissing, PA 19610

Strategic Thinking

Copyright Notice

© Copyright 2010 ALERA Publishing Group

All Rights Reserved. No part of this book may be reproduced or transmitted in any form or by any means electronic or mechanical, including photocopying, recording, or by any information storage or retrieval system, without written permission of the ALERA Publishing Group, Inc., except for inclusion of brief quotations in a review.

Published by ALERA Publishing Group, Inc. Wyomissing, PA 19610

Printed in the United States of America

ISBN 978-0-557-53240-7

This Book is intended to support our Strategic Thinking Webinar. For more information, please visit our website at http://www.aleragroup.com

Strategic Thinking

Introduction

The ability to plan long-term while maximizing performance in the short-term is a must for managers. Strategic thinking will help you map out the route to success and build your analytic and team planning skills

Strategic thinking is the acquired habit of developing and analyzing every decision made after taking into consideration the present and future conditions, the desired outcome and the expected results. Strategic thinking involves identifying challenges and solving problems that arise by assessing these in a broader framework. Critical skills are required for determining what you aim at achieving in the future, and how to work towards it.

Defining Strategy

A strategy is a declaration of intent, defining where you want to be in the long-term. Strategy was once as "the art of planning and directing large military movements and the operations of war." In business, a strategy maps out the future setting out which products and services you will take to which markets – and how.

Having a strategy enables you to ensure that day-to-day decisions fit in with the long-term interests of the organization. Without a strategy, decisions made today could have a negative impact on future results. A strategy encourages everyone to work together to achieve common aims Most organizations have a strategic plan at the highest level, but some do not communicate it all the way down.

Today's business environment puts pressure on people to complete urgent tasks, meet day-to-day objectives, and overcome short-term problems. This is called short-term or operational planning, and it too often takes precedence over planning for the future. Strategy concerns itself with what is ahead, looking at where you are going, and how you will get there. Even if you already know which products and services you are taking to which markets, you still need a strategy to make it happen.

To get the best from your people, it is important to work within a clear framework that details how they will be expected to help you develop and implement a strategic plan. The STOP™ program is just such a framework. Think of the STOP™ methods and processes as a map that the team can follow to achieve success. The STOP™ process helps you to encourage the team to pull together and work to a common Objective. It also helps you promote their personal development by teaching them to think strategically.

Examining the Process

There are three distinct phases to developing a new strategy:

1. Analysis
2. Planning
3. Implementation.

It is vital to devote time and effort to the first two stages, but also to maintain momentum throughout the implementation to ensure ultimate success.

Analysis
During the analysis phase, you will collect as much background information as you can to help you make informed decisions. This stage is crucial because the facts you have at hand will influence the direction you decide to take. You will analyze what is happening inside your organization, looking carefully at aspects of your own and other parts of the company that may influence the plan. Your aim is to draw a clear statement of the strengths and weaknesses of your position as well as a list of opportunities for the future.

Planning
Once you have gathered all of the necessary facts, the nest step is to make strategic decisions that will bring you closer to your overall aim. You will need to take into account where you have advantages over the competition and establish the boundaries within which you will operate.

The decisions you reach will help you to establish your future financial position and work out a realistic budget.

Implementation
During the final phase of developing a strategy you will determine, on the basis of your analysis, what you are going to do and how you are going to do it. It may be possible to achieve your aims with little change to the way your team works. On the other hand, you may find that success depends on making far-reaching changes and learning new skills. Do not make the mistake of working so hard on the analysis phase that planning and

Strategic Thinking

implementation receive less overall effort –this will result in less than effective strategies and incomplete implementation.

Strategic Thinking

Thinking Short-Term & Long-Term

The ability to differentiate between short-term and long-term thinking and strike a balance between the two is an integral part of strategy. Understand the importance of both in strategic planning and you will find it easier to achieve the right combination of the two.

Short-term planning deals with the here and now or a few weeks hence, while long-term thinking takes you far into the future. If you focus entirely on short-term success, you risk long-term failure.

Striking the right balance between short-term and long-term thinking takes effort and discipline. If you cancel a strategy meeting, it will have no short-term impact. It becomes clear that unless a team is determined to give time to strategic issues, short-term operational tasks will always take priority.

Strategy is a continuous process; even when your plan becomes operational, you cannot neglect future planning. Set aside one day each month to discuss maintaining and developing the plan with the team. The most successful manager allow at least ½ day per week to implement the strategic part of their jobs.

Preparing for Strategic Success

An effective strategic plan has accurate information, strong ideas, and committed people at its core. Involve the right people from the outset, and then encourage them to research facts, and brainstorm for ideas to achieve the best possible plan.

An effective team is essential for a successful strategy. Involve the whole team early on in the planning process so that they feel part of the process. Managers sometimes avoid team planning at this stage because they are not sure that all the people involved will play a significant role in the implementation of the strategy at a later date. Team planning is always useful; it allows you to assess team members as well as giving them the chance to decide if they are happy to work within the new strategy as it develops, or whether they feel they could make a greater contribution in another environment.

Strategic Thinking

People with an interest in or influence on the new strategy are known as "stakeholders." Foster good relations with them, since they often provide experience or information, or can help with the analysis and decision making. Strategic planning often requires people form different areas of the organization to formulate a plan together. This spirit of cooperation produces the best results.

Once you have developed your strategy, it is vital that the team does not start to lose interest during implementation. It is your role as manager to ensure that everyone understands the importance of the long-term strategy and is dedicated to making it happen. First, everyone should agree that a new strategy is needed. Second, everyone involved in the strategic process must feel confident that, guided by their manager, they have developed the right plan. Third, everyone must feel personally committed to making the strategy happen. Make the team aware that operational pressures are not an excuse for missing target dates involved in implementing the strategy.

The importance of basing your strategy on the right information cannot be stressed enough. Poor data may lead to a crises when the correct facts come to light, meaning the whole plan may need to be changed. The same goes for using out-of-date facts or failing to collect all the information. Bear in minds that a poor strategic plan can lead to long-term failure and disappointing short-term results.

Successful strategies must have strong factual foundations. Relying on guess work or estimates could lead to a strategy collapsing, so avoid these at all costs, no matter how convincing they appear. Get all relevant information before reaching a conclusion. The STOP™ process will help you do this.

Coming up with ideas is paramount in strategic planning, whether it is thinking of key trends to be monitored, pinpointing possible choices that could be made, or suggesting new an innovative ways to gain a competitive advantage. Throughout the strategic process, you and your team should meet regularly to brainstorm ideas.

Strategic Thinking

Characteristics of Strategic Thinkers

Important characteristics of the strategic thinker include:

Adaptable — The strategic thinker must be flexible. Instead of having a plan carved in stone with the inflexibility of stone, The strategic thinker designs a loose framework of how the business will run and makes adjustments as things arise. It is important not to use reactive knee-jerk ideas but remain open to changing direction as needs dictate.

Flexibility — Strategic thinkers plan flexible tactics by constantly reviewing the progress made and changing plans to handle current circumstances. It is critical that they benchmark their thinking and utilize any developing opportunity that will help to achieve the set goals. They must take the initiative, anticipate changes, and be prepared to deal with any challenges that may result. Rather than being overwhelmed by changes, strategic thinkers must adjust their thinking and formulate other contingency plans.

Perceptive — Strategic thinkers need to be subtle and recognize emerging clues that will help in plot a course for the future direction and taking advantage of opportunities. They must listen while other people are talking and make observations which will help in decision making.

Vision Oriented — Strategic thinkers need to have the ability to create a detailed vision, by stating the goals and objectives that will be achieved within a given time line. They must be able to formulate an action plan for each goal by breaking it down into smaller tasks.

Disciplined — Strategic thinkers must be patient and avoid making hasty judgments, decisions or conclusions. They must be mindful that time is required to achieve the defined vision. Strategic thinkers should not abandon their plans half-way because of challenges, rather, they should persevere until they are accomplished.

Strategic Thinking

Fact – Based While goals and ambitions are important,, it is more essential to remember the facts. Strengths and weaknesses such as competition, the local economy, overhead and ability to employ enough workers all come into play when it comes to strategic thinking. Aligning goals and desires with the facts as they currently exist are critical if the goal setting is to be realistic and attainable.

Purpose of Strategic Thinking

The purpose of Strategic Thinking is to create a strategy that is a coherent, unifying, integrative framework for decisions especially about direction of the business and resource utilization. To accomplish this, Strategic Thinking uses internal and external data, a combination of opinions and perceptions. It is a conscious and proactive effort that defines the competitive environment to gain sustainable corporate strategic advantage. Effective strategy should be the key outcome of any strategic thinking process

Importance of Developing Critical Thinking Skills

Strategic thinking requires critical thinking skills which involve seeing things as they are rather than how they make you feel. It requires that you evaluate things slowly and methodically in order to truly evaluate them rather than making spur-of-the-moment emotional judgments.

Critical thinking is a form of higher level thinking, sometimes called the scientific method of thinking. Critical thinking helps you make decisions by analyzing and evaluating your facts. Improving your critical thinking skills helps you improve your strategic thinking in order to make more intelligent decisions.

Critical thinking skills are noticeably different from the ability to recall facts. Recalling information is one thing, however, critical thinking skills involve the ability to synthesize and process information. More than just knowing casual facts, a critical thinker must be able to look at facts and understand their significance. This is an essential skill as we can be overwhelmed by information every day and it is up to us to "filter the data," using critical thinking skills in order to consider, process and evaluate the facts that are before us.

Observe the finer details of everything, including both tangible and intangible things; if someone tells you something, consider everything about what they said, the way they said it

Strategic Thinking

and what caused them to say it. In other words, to be a successful critical thinker you must focus on the context of what they are saying.

Consider things from various angles. Everything has a different point of view; your view of, , an accident is different from someone across the street, partly because you are standing in different locations and looking at it from different angles, and partly because you both likely had dissimilar experiences with accidents in the past. So, to think critically you need to always consider the fact that everything looks different from a different angle.

Set criteria on which you will judge things. Critical thinking requires understanding things objectively rather than subjectively. Follow the criteria you set when evaluating anything. This basically removes your emotions from the equation, which is important because critical thinking is about viewing things as they are rather than how they affect you or make you feel.

Logic and reasoning are central components of critical thinking. Using strong logic and reasoning helps the thinker assemble thoughts and arrive at suitable solutions. A thinker, for example, may consider different ways to rob a bank, but fail to comprehend that bank robbery is an irrational measure, logically speaking. Logic and reasoning help the thinker increase his/her concept of empathy and strengthen considerations of ethics and morality.

Insight is another essential element of critical thinking, it is founded on the personal experience a thinker brings to the process of critical thinking. Personal experience in operations, for example, broadens a thinker's perspective and understanding of the issues and complications that can arise in a process. Using insight as a tool to measure and evaluate critical thinking decisions is an invaluable concept for expanding evaluation skills.

Learning to Think Strategically

In order to Think Strategically, you need to:

1. Analyze the current situation in terms of the status quo. Strategic thinking skills require that you critically examine how things have always been done in order to determine if that is the way things should be done. Strategic thinkers must be willing to look outside of the box to find creative and more effective ways of doing things.

Strategic Thinking

2. Look at the big picture and see the forest, not the trees. Do not be mired down by the details of managing day-to-day issues. Look at the organization as a whole in order to assess important characteristics and areas of opportunity.

3. Focus on the future. Strategic thinking is goal oriented and guided by a vision for the future of a company. When you are developing strategies for business growth, those strategies must have clearly defined goals that contribute to the overall vision for the company.

4. Consider external forces when you develop a strategic plan. Governmental regulations, legal developments, market conditions, economic factors and technological developments can all affect how you plan for the future.

5. Benchmark your industry to get feedback. Conduct market research, particularly in product-driven industries, in order help you match the vision for your company to consumer expectations.

6. Constantly check the facts. While strategic thinking involves making predictions about the future, those predictions must be realistic. Gather hard data, such as your organizations financial reports and analysis of your industry, to update your predictions and help develop your goals based in reality.

7. Consider the organizational structure of your business and evaluate how that structure fits into your strategies for the future. You may have to reorganize in order to achieve your goals.

8. Anticipate any possible challenges. It is an important part of thinking strategically to be able to predict what issues will arise and to devise a plan for confronting those issues in advance.

Strategic Thinking for Operations and Projects

Figure 1: The STOP™ Cycle

Strategic Thinking

The Strategic Thinking for Operations and Projects (STOP™) program was designed to help you build a strong business case for change. This program will guide you through a proven framework for developing strategy. The STOP™ Cycle consists of the following steps:

- Assessment of the Situation
- Objective(s)
- Strategy(ies)
- Action Planning
- Action Taking
- Gauging Impact

Assessment of the Situation (Situation Analysis)

The assessment of the situation is where critical questions must be answered
- What is happening?
- Why?
- What does it mean to us? What is the problem or opportunity?
- What is the scope?

This analysis is the key to the STOP™ process. If it is correct, all that follows tends to be correct. If it is wrong, all that follows tends to be wrong. A thorough situation analysis must include the following elements:
- Problem opportunity statement
- Frame of reference
- External market factors
- Internal resource factors
- Thoroughness and iteration
- Synthesis (analysis, sorting, and organization).

Strategic Thinking

Situational Analysis is where critical information is gathered, analyzed, sifted, sorted, re-analyzed, organized, and connected/linked.

In order to identify...	Which answers the question of...?
The root causes (driving forces) in the situation, and	"What is happening?"
How these causes/forces are interconnected, or linked, to each other.	"Why? Why? Why? Why? Why?"
The significance/importance/impact of the causes/forces	"So what?" "What does it mean to us?

Table 1

Focus (what are the root causes and/or driving forces) and linkage (how are these related to each other) are critical to situational analysis. It is difficult to achieve linkage of the six key components of the STOP™ process, if the analysis is not focused and vice-versa.

Problem/ Opportunity Statements

A problem/opportunity statement is the typical starting point of a situational analysis. A problem statement is a straight forward declaration of the core issue(s) that must be addressed in order to resolve the situation.

An opportunity statement is a straight forward declaration for taking advantage of the key potential within the situation. It requires action.

A problem/opportunity statement is typically phrased as a question. It is likely the statement will be modified or altered significantly as you collect and interpret data and draw conclusions regarding the situation.

In some cases, you may be given a tentative objective, target, or strategy – which you must convert, or translate into a problem/opportunity statement

- A well written problem/ opportunity statement should be:
- Understandable
- Clearly articulated
- Focused (limited to clearly defined parameters).

Strategic Thinking

The problem/ opportunity statement provides focus (direction, scope, breadth, and depth) for the situational; analysis. If the statement is not clearly defined, the situation analysis will lack focus.

Once the situation analysis is complete, the problem/ opportunity statement should be "answered" by the objective. The problem/ opportunity statement should be rechecked several times during the situational analysis process for validity.

Frame of Reference

The frame of reference sets the boundaries for approaching the situational analysis and the rest of the STOP™ process. It puts a frame around what is, and is not, included in the situational analysis and is a powerful part of the STOP™ set-up. When a frame of reference is not clear, it can cause additional and unnecessary work. When it is clearly focused, it will help you decide which information should be considered and analyzed.

A clearly established frame of reference:

- Defines the parameters of what should – and should not be – included in the analysis
- Must reflect the point of focus identified in the problem/opportunity statement:
- Wide enough to include all relevant data
- Narrow enough to exclude all irrelevant data
- Includes a reference to time (nest 6 months, over 5 years, etc.)

This parameter can be defined by:

- Geography
- Customer/consumer
- Product/service attributes

Strategic Thinking

Supplemental Framework

To enhance the situational analysis, use a supplemental framework such as a cause-and-effect diagram as shown in **Error! Reference source not found.**, to collect data. The frame work for the diagram could be

Framework	Description
4–C's	1. Company 2. Competitors 3. Customers 4. Consumers
4–P's	1. Product 2. Price 3. Promotion 4. Place
7–S's	1. Strategy 2. Structure 3. Systems 4. Staff 5. Skills 6. Style 7. Shared Values
Others	There are many categories you can use the ones above are the most common.

Table 2:

Strategic Thinking

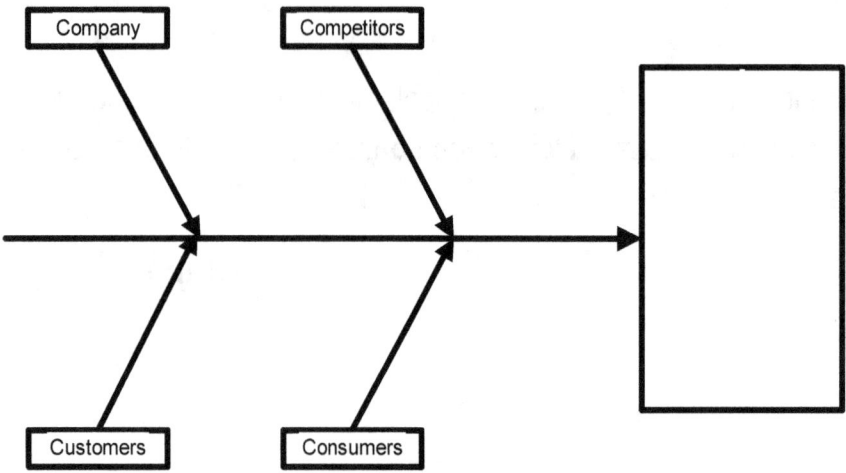

Figure 2: Blank Cause & Effect Diagram

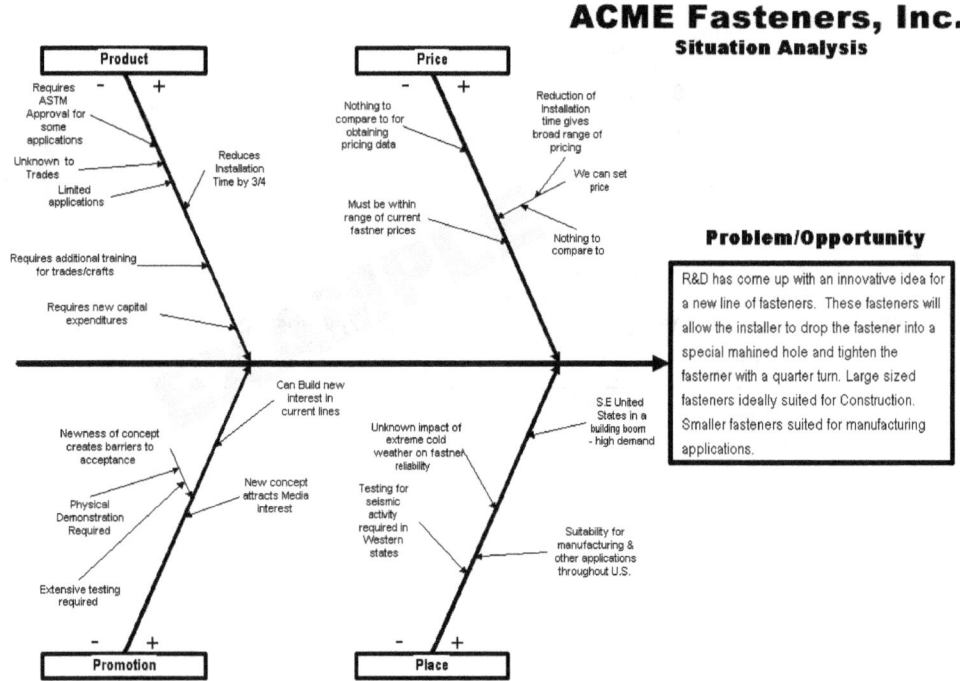

Figure 3: Example of Situation Analysis Diagram

Strategic Thinking

SWOT Analysis

A SWOT Analysis is drawn from key take-aways in the situation analysis. There should not be any "new news". You should develop a SWOT Analysis for you and for your competitors

Figure 4: SWOT Factors

The SWOT Analysis should be done for you and your competitors.

Internal Situation	External Situation
Strength and Weaknesses are derived from the analysis of the internal situation (Direct control/influence):	Opportunities and Threats are generally derived from the analysis of the external situation (No/little control/influence):
<ul><li>Finances</li><li>Profitability</li><li>Cross-functional resources & relationships</li><li>Organization dynamics</li><li>Other relevant internal factors/categories.</li></ul>	<ul><li>Business/industry environment</li><li>Competition</li><li>Customer/trade</li><li>Consumer</li><li>Other relevant external factors/categories.</li></ul>

Table 3

Strategic Thinking

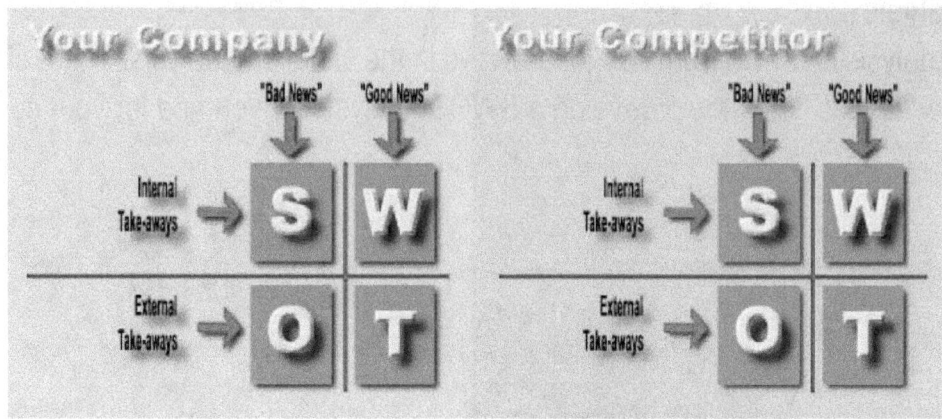

Figure 5: SWOT Comparison

In making use of SWOT Analysis, start with overall strengths and weaknesses, then find the best combination of relative strengths (and the absence of critical weaknesses) to use against specific competitors in specific markets

In developing a SWOT Analysis, either for yourself or a competitor, consider these points:

- Generally, even in most complex situation, there should be no more than 3–4 conclusions for each category of a SWOT.
- Both strengths and weaknesses are internal; they are within the direct control of the company
- Both opportunities and threats are usually external; they are outside the direct control of the company
- By definition, a key point for one category cannot be a key point for another category
- Strengths and weaknesses are relative and have limits. No strength or weakness applies against all competitors in all market situations

Comparing the Competitors' SWOT Analysis to your own SWOT Analysis can be very enlightening in determining how to address the issue identified in the problem/opportunity statement.

These comparisons can also help to identify true strengths and opportunities for you and the competition. For example, if your analysis identified the same strength for you and a key competitor, it is possible that it is not a strength for either of you – but is actually a requirement for competing in this market

Business Implications, Key Leverage Points & SCAs

Your SWOT and your competitors SWOT can be further synthesized into:

- Business Implications
- Key Leverage Points
- Significant Competitive Advantage

Business Implications (BIs) are:

- Negative or potentially negative take-aways so significant, that they must be addressed in strategies and/or plans. If not your proposed solutions can not go forward
- Derived from your *Weaknesses* and *Threats* and the competitor's *Strengths* and *Opportunities*
- Provide a complete answer to this statement:
    - To win, we must (address; fix; repair; correct) …
    - In order not to lose, we must

Key Leverage Points (KLPs) are:

- Combinations of positive (or potentially positive), take-aways that provide you with greater opportunities than the competition. They can be build upon, extended, or expanded
- Usually derived from your *Strengths* and *Opportunities* and your competitors' *Weaknesses* and *Threats*
- Provide a complete answer to the statement:
    - "By leveraging… we will achieve our objective."

A Significant Competitive Advantage:

- Is a unique combination of factors that gives you/your company advantage over the competition
- Is a compelling reason to be (or not to be) in business

Strategic Thinking

- Must be strategic and significant
- Helps if you are first
- Several Key Leverage Points (KLPs) can be an SCA

SCAs can be, but are not limited to:

- Technology/patent
- Geography
- Cost advantage/manufacturing process
- People skills/experience
- Brand name
- Relationships with key constituents
- Timing
- Trademark
- Product differential
- Synergy/Combination of factors
- Unique selling proposition
- Core competencies

Figure 6: Summarizing Significant Competitive Advantage

In identifying and/or creating an SCA, there are five(5) options:

1. You already have one
2. You can get one soon
3. you do not have one, but can build one
4. You do not have one, you cannot get one, but there is still a very strong compelling reason to compete in this arena (competitive response, complete portfolio, etc.)

5. You do not have one, you cannot get one, you face a competitor who has one … Maybe you shouldn't be in this arena

SCA – real or potential – can be identified by exploring the relationships between the business Implications and the Key Leverage Points

Conclusions – Implications

The final part of the Situation Analysis are the:

Conclusions   The most important "learnings" or "take-aways" from the assessment that bear on what needs to be done

Implications   What the conclusions specifically suggest for our response to this situation – the "*so what*" that points to what we need to consider doing

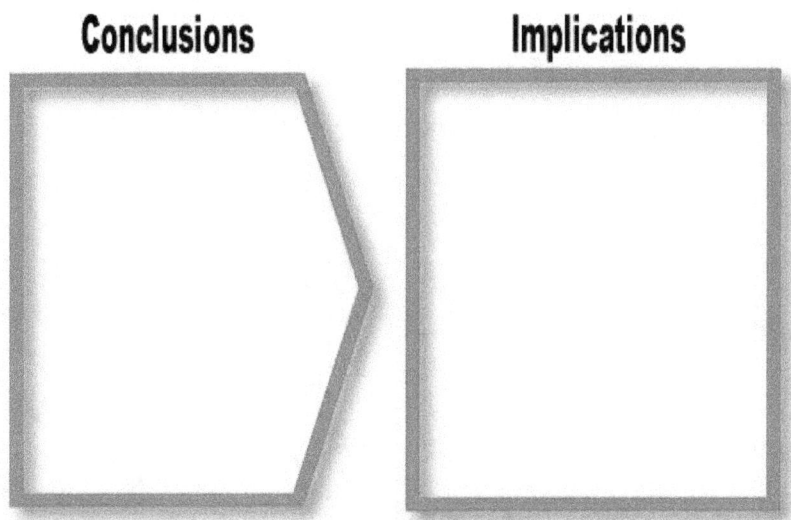

Figure 7: Conclusions

The following example illustrates the relationship between Facts, implications and conclusions:

FACT: Profit margin was 15% (Sales were $1,000,000, profits were $150,000

FACT: Average profit margin for competitors is 20%

Strategic Thinking

CONCLUSION: We are underperforming vs. Competition

IMPLICATIONS: Change is needed

Strategic Thinking

Objectives (Goals)

The objective must answer the question: "*What does success look like?*" The situation analysis describes the current state of affairs, while the objective describes the future.

The objective must answer the question: "*What does success look like?*" The situation analysis describes the current state of affairs, while the objective describes the future.

Developing an Objective

The first step in developing an objective is often a vision statement. It should begin with a qualitative statement; it should also address the situat5ion analysis and problem/opportunity statement.

The objective should be SMART:

- Specific
- Measurable
- Agreed-Upon
- Realistic
- Time-Specific

Figure 8: SMART Objectives

Strategic Thinking

The following are examples of objectives:

A weak objective: Become the market leader

A little better: Become the market leader in Eastern United States by achieving 30% market share by 2005

The best objective: Become the market leader in Eastern United States by 2005 as measured by an increase from 20% in 2004 to 30%, volume from 100MM to 150MM and an IFO of 15% per year from $12MM to $20MM.

When the timeframe for achieving these results extends beyond 12 months, the objective may require several benchmarks of key measures. For example:

Year 1 From 2 to 5% share at 5% profitability
Year 2 From 5 to 10% share at 12% profitability
Year 3 From 10 to 17% share at 20% profitability

Ideas for Measures

Accurate appropriate measures are crucial when writing objectives that address all the major aspects of the situation analysis and problem/opportunity statement> Consider measures of:

QUANTITY		
• Profitability	• Volume	• Turns
• Revenues	• Share	• Turnover
• Tonnage	• Margin	• Ratios/percentages
QUALITY		
• Serviceability	• Consumer feedback	• Complaints/ compliments
• Durability	• Referrals	
• Reliability	• Survey ratings	
COST		
• Dollars	• Return ratio	• Rework
• Time	• Savings	• Scrap
• Efficiency	• Expense	• Returns
TIME		

Strategic Thinking

• Completion date time • Phase dates	• Cycle time • Frequency	• Through-put • Lead-time

Strategy(ies)

The situation analysis describes where you are. The objective states where you want to be. And the strategies show how to get from where you are to where you want to be.

The strategy or strategies must answer the question: "How will success be achieved?" Thus a strategy provides a broad, planned, direct approach to addressing the problem/opportunity and achieving the objective. It leverages the key strengths and or resources uncovered in the situation analysis.

In particular, the strategies must link to the objective and the situation analysis, use KLPs, resolve BI's and leverage the SCA.

Developing the best strategy or strategies, includes consideration of the following factors:

- The more complex the situation, the more likely the need for multiple strategies
- Use creativity and innovation to uncover approaches beyond the obvious
- Identify alternatives/contingency strategies that can be implemented should a preferred strategy fail
- Think through the rational for a given preferred strategy – why is it the best approach? What other approaches were seriously considered and why they were rejected?

Strategy Building Ideas

There are several ways to transform meaningful insights into appropriate strategies:

- Study your SWOT, BIs, KLPs, and SCA:
- How can you use your strength, to achieve your opportunities, negate your weaknesses, and address your threats?
- Said another way, how can you use your KLP and SCA to address the problem/opportunity while overcoming and negating the BIs?
- Compare your SWOT to the competitor's SWOTs:
- How can you leverage your strengths against their weaknesses?
- How can you use their threats and weaknesses to your advantage?

Strategic Thinking

- Based on their SWOTs, what strategies are the competitors using? What alternatives are available to you?

Plan of Action

Plans of action are specific actions to achieve objectives. There should always be one set of plans for each strategy. The plan must answer the question "What are the details to make it happen?" plans specify the activities and resources required to bring each strategy to life and to achieve the objective. Plans are the detailed "blueprints" that must be followed during the "Taking Action step

Structure of Plans

Plans must indicate:
- What needs to be done (activities, tasks, action steps)
- Who is responsible (person, function, department, etc.)
- When (timing, dates)
- How much (costs, resources-all aspects of the budget)
- Milestones and/or contingencies

Taking Action

Strategic Thinking

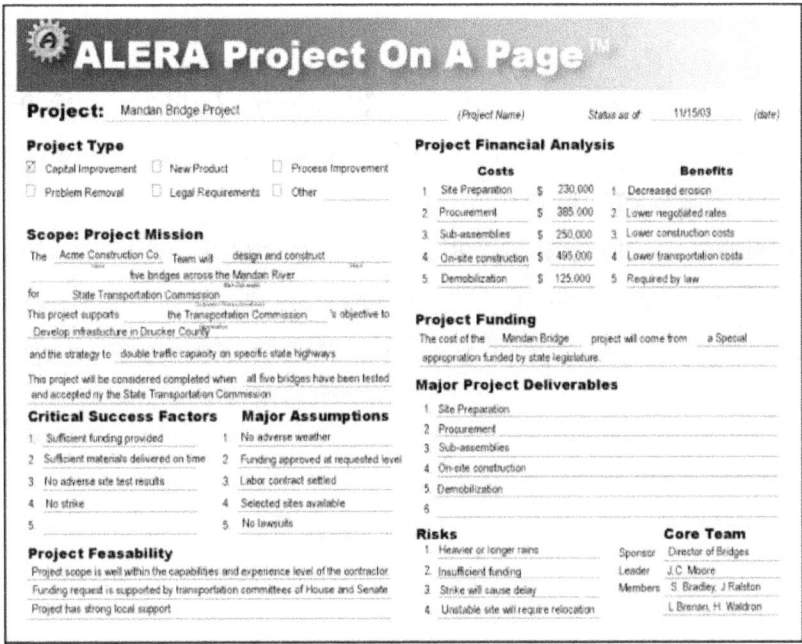

Figure 9: Typical Action Plan

Strategic Thinking

Taking action sets the strategy into motion through careful attention to each detail laid out in the plans. It converts analysis and planning into action and results. During the taking action step, give attention to the following points:

- Monitor unfolding results – expected and unexpected
- Keep contingency plans adjusted and ready
- Keep all key players – internal and external– involved and informed
- Communicate!

Gauging Impact

Gauging impact identifies and monitors (tracks) the key measures used to validate interim and final results, and what is happening in the current/new situation. Gauging impact answers the question: "How do we know we're winning?" "What are the results?"

The primary elements that need to be tracked can be found in the objective (What are the critical measures?) and the situation analysis (What are the root causes/driving forces? What else might change that would significantly alter the situation?" Gauging impact tracks the factors critical to the problem/opportunity at hand. It is not to be confused with monitoring plan milestones. There should be one set of tracking measures for the entire STOP™ analysis... not for each strategy

Typically, the primary elements that need to be tracked can be found in the objective (What are the critical measures?) and the situational analysis (what are the root causes/driving forces? What else might change that would significantly alter the situation?)

Considerations

Gauging impact must consider:

- What needs to be measured? (Measure)
- How should each be measured? (Source)
- Who should take the measurements? (Responsibility)
- When or how often? (Timing)

Strategic Thinking

- What are the targets/expectation? (Targets)

Typically, for complex business situation that involve a number of functional areas and a variety of external factors, consideration should be given to developing tracking measures for such key areas as:

- Industry trends
- Competitive actions
- Customer/trade dynamics
- Consumer preferences
- Government actions
- Market share
- Volume
- Financial targets

In addition to these "complex" measures for gauging impact, there can be any number of other measures required to monitor the specific details of the situation analysis and the plans. For example, each significant action step may require its own tracking measure that assures on-time, efficient and effective completion.

Strategic Thinking

Resources

Topic	See Page
Books	30
Training Programs	36
Services	37

ALERA Group Website

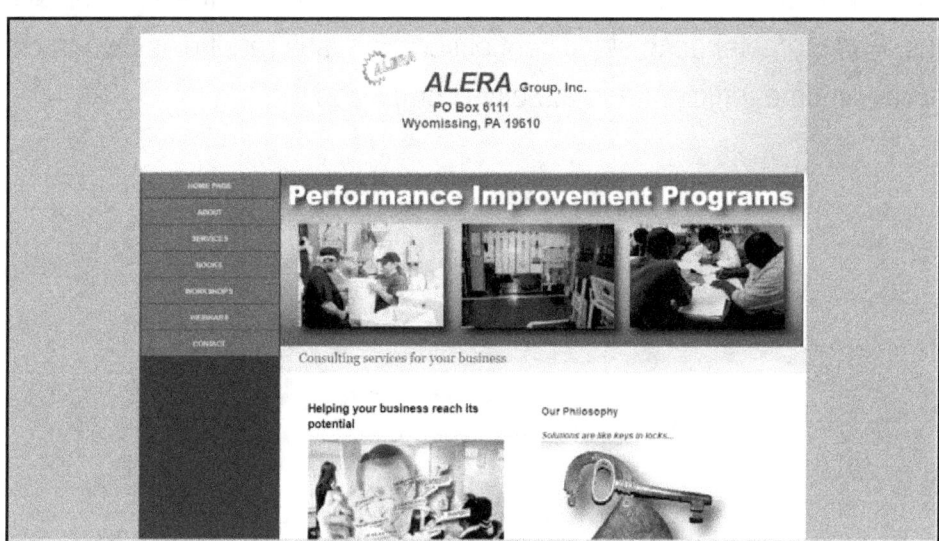

http://www.aleragroup.com

Strategic Thinking

Books From ALERA Publishing Group

5S Topics

Planning & Implementing 5S

Paperback	$24.99
Hard Cover	$36.53

The Planning & Implementing 5S program shows you how to organize a Performance Improvement Steering Team, how to analyze the workplace, how to plan a facility-wide improvement program, and how to sustain your efforts.

5S Workbook

Paperback	$14.48

The 5S workbook is the companion to Planning and Implementing 5S by Brice Alvord. It provides the tools used in the ALERA workshop.

Auditing Your 5S Program

Paperback	$14.99

The 5S audit is critical to the success of your 5S program. It is often overlooked or considered an unnecessary extra expense. The audit validates the accountability of the target area owners for complying with 5S plans. Without the audit, the program slowly withers away and becomes ineffective. A close look at 5S failures will reveal a lack of or an ineffective auditing program. This book explains how to conduct a proper 5S audit.

Building A 5Steam

Paperback	$17.99

Building A 5S team explains what a 5S Team needs to know in order to function properly. This book covers how to form a team, write a charter, how to run the team once it is created. this book provides a foundation for teamwork and continuous improvement activities.

Strategic Planning For 5S

Paperback	$30.51

Strategic Planning for 5S is intended for managers and steering committee members who are considering the implementation of a 5S program. It shows how to apply Strategic Thinking to the 5S planning and implementation process and develop a strong business case for change

Continued on next page

Strategic Thinking

Error! Use the Home tab to apply Map Title to the text that you want to appear here., Continued

Creating A Performance Based Culture In Your Workplace

CD: $34.99

Creating a Performance Based Culture in your workplace is a nuts and bolts approach to planning and implementing a performance based continuous improvement program for your facility. It shows you how to incorporate strategic planning and business needs analysis into a strong program that addresses your business needs and related performance issues. It shows you how to create a strong business case for change and how to create structured on job training designed to carry out that business case. Filled with illustrations, charts and procedures. Includes state of the art tools to help improve your organization's performance and improve your bottom line.

Training

How to Train People On The Job

Paperback $18.53

NEW and REVISED workbook for Training On the Job Trainers. Covers adult learning theory, why shadow training does not work, how to perform a simple job/task analysis, how to develop trainer's guides and teach using the Four Step Method

Performance Based Training

Paperback $21.95

This book is intended as a guide to Performance Based Instructional Design. It covers how to conduct an effective Training Analysis including Job/Task Analysis, how to identify and define realistic competencies and instructional objectives and how to organize analysis data into a performance based training design. The book also explains how to develop important training documents including trainer's guides and lesson plans, participant manuals, and support materials including training and job aids and other media. Performance Based Training: Building a Competent Workforce is intended for the training professional as well as those people who have been given a training assignment.

Continued on next page

Strategic Thinking

Training, Continued

Advanced Instructional Design
Paperback $21.95

Advanced Instructional design focuses on the steps required to develop a performance based training design. Chapters include information conducting a Job Task Analysis and the Design of the training program. Other topics include defining competencies, conducting a DACUM, writing performance based objectives, developing criterion tests, Sequencing training elements, and writing a training blueprint. This book does not cover the development of training materials that will be addressed in another book yet to be published.

One Point Lessons
Paperback $11.94

This book is a training workbook for developing One-Point Lessons. It is designed to provide clear and simple explanations of procedures and techniques to quickly create short, cost effective training materials.

Operations Performance Improvement
Paperback $21.59
Hard Cover $36.30

Fundamentals of Operations Performance Analysis shows your OPI team how to develop effective solutions to persistent performance problems. Your team will learn how to isolate and understand the root cause of defects and failures within equipment mechanisms and peripheral systems. They will learn how to apply a systematic approach for effectively controlling those causes.

Overall Equipment Effectiveness
Paperback $17.56

Overall Equipment Effectiveness (OEE) is a universal measurement that has been used worldwide for over 10 years. It is a formula to measure the efficiency of production line equipment. In short, OEE measures the ratio of first-pass acceptable product actually produced to the theoretical amount that could be produced under optimal conditions.

Strategic Thinking

Continued on next page

Strategic Thinking

Error! Use the Home tab to apply Map Title to the text that you want to appear here., Continued

Strategic Thinking

Paperback $13.16

Strategic Thinking for Operations & Projects focuses on how to build a strategic based business case for change. It is a powerful communications tool for getting projects approved.

Fundamentals of Project Management

Paperback $16.38

Project Management Fundamentals covers the fundamental skills required to plan and implement project. It is intended for new project managers and managers with little or no project management experience.

Strategic Thinking

Training Programs From ALERA Group

How To Train People On The Job

A 2 Day Hands-on Workshop that teaches your participants how to conduct On Job Training using the Four Step Method of Instruction.

Planning & Implementing 5S Workshop

A 3 Day Hands-On Workshop that teaches your participants how to plan and implement a basic 5S program. They will actually begin implementing 5S in a target area of your facility.

Team Based Problem Solving

A 2 Day Hands-on Workshop to teach your teams how to work together to identify and solve real problems in the workplace. Teams will address n actual problem and apply the tools to solve it.

Project Management Workshop

A 2 Day Hands-on Workshop that teaches the fundamentals of project management. Participants develop all of the elements of a project.

Overall Equipment Effectiveness

A 1 Day Hands-on Workshop to teach your participants what Overall Equipment Effectiveness is and how to calculate it accurately.

Try Z Seminar

A 2 ½ to 4 Day Hands-on Workshop from QCDSM Systems, Inc. See QCDSM Program Information on page **Error! Bookmark not defined.**.

Strategic Thinking

Services From ALERA Group

Introduction	The ALERA Consulting Group exists to assist you in improving all areas of performance in your organization. We have a variety of state of the art tools and processes to help you identify performance needs and relate them to business practices and strategies.
Strategic Thinking	ALERA helps you develop strategic thinking in your organization; We conduct a strategic thinking workshop for selected members of your management team. We coach them through the application of the Strategic Thinking model to help them develop comprehensive and effective business cases for change within your organization.
Team Building	ALERA helps you design and deliver the right customized team development program, team building event, corporate retreat, or executive retreat that will improve your team's effectiveness, collaboration skills, and team-based results.
New Leader Assimilation	ALERA's Leader Assimilation program is based on the process designed by Kaiser Aluminum. Kaiser discovered that it normally took an incoming manager six months to become fully productive. The process was designed to reduce this amount of organizational down-time.
High Impact Change Management	ALERA's High Impact Change Management is a 3 phase organizational design program that assesses the organization with a performance audit, rationalizes change, and develops a comprehensive design. ALERA provides: design team formation and training, strategy focused design, alignment of the organization for maximum effectiveness, and building an empowered organization.
Asset Effectiveness (Focused Equipment Improvement)	ALERA helps your Operations Improvement Team develop the skills to address chronic equipment problems that hinder your profitability and overall performance. We provide workshops o help your team succeed. We evaluate your team's performance and coach individual members and your management team.

Continued on next page

Strategic Thinking

Error! Use the Home tab to apply Map Title to the text that you want to appear here., Continued

Training Analysis	ALERA conducts or teaches your team to conduct a variety of training analysis including: training needs analysis, job/task analysis, cost benefit analysis, Our training professionals conduct training effectiveness audits, subject matter interviews, and individual performance evaluations.
Workplace Organization (5S planning and implementation)	ALERA helps you analyze your needs, design a program, plan 5S implementation, evaluate the progress of your program, perform 5S audits, coach your management team on implementation problems and opportunities.
Project Management	ALERA has experienced project managers who can assist you with keeping your performance improvement project or training project on schedule and under budget. We address your organizational needs and support consulting efforts with comprehensive training programs for your team as needed.
Technical Writing and Instructional Design and Development	ALERA can provide you with technical writers to help you develop standard operating procedures, lockout/tagout procedures technical documentation, training manuals, detailed process sheets.

Strategic Thinking

Strategic Thinking

Strategic Thinking